S0-ENV-654

THE FORGOTTEN TROLLEY

WELLS-FARWELL

NORTH

Written by Mary Ruth Weaver
Illustrations by Jeff Eckman

Copyright © 2008 Mary Ruth Weaver
All rights reserved.

ISBN: 1-4392-3186-9
ISBN-13: 9781439231869
Library of Congress Control Number: 2008906288

DEDICATION

This book is dedicated to my husband, Gary Heiligenthal, whose fascination, love, and knowledge of trolley cars inspired me to write this book. He enjoys meeting with his buddy, Jack Gervais and other members of the Milwaukee Electric Railway and Historical Society in Milwaukee, Wisconsin to reminisce, discuss, and share stories about trolley cars. My brother, Kenneth Weaver, is named as one of the trolley cars, as well as Gary's cousin, August Schepker. My two sisters, Diana Huddleston, and Lori Hawbaker share a part in this story as passengers. I know they all will enjoy reading about The Forgotten Trolley.

ACKNOWLEDGEMENT

I would like to thank my agent and daughter, Vikki Majors, for all her support and assistance in encouraging me to pursue my passion for writing. Her resourceful endeavors retained an up and coming illustrator, Jeff Eckman, who has worked with me to produce a book for all ages. Many thanks to both of them for taking this leap of faith with me.

HONORARY ACKNOWLEDGEMENT

I would be remiss if I did not pay homage to two people who influenced my writing.

First, to Mrs. Clevenger, my First Grade Teacher in Knoxville, Tennessee, who instilled within me my love of reading. Secondly, to David Coy, Professor Emeritus, Division of Communications at Arizona Western College, Yuma, Arizona. His encouragement and instruction provided the impetus needed to achieve my goal.

He sat very still. He was very, very quiet. He knew no one was ever going to visit him again.

Then, he sighed, and a little tear trickled down his cheek. It rolled down the front of him and onto the ground. It landed in the puddle with all the other tears he had cried.

You see, this little fellow was a trolley car. His name was Al. At least that's what his best friend, Gary, used to call him whenever he took a ride on him.

Gary would hop on the trolley, drop a nickel in the fare box, give it a little pat, and say, "Hello, Al!"

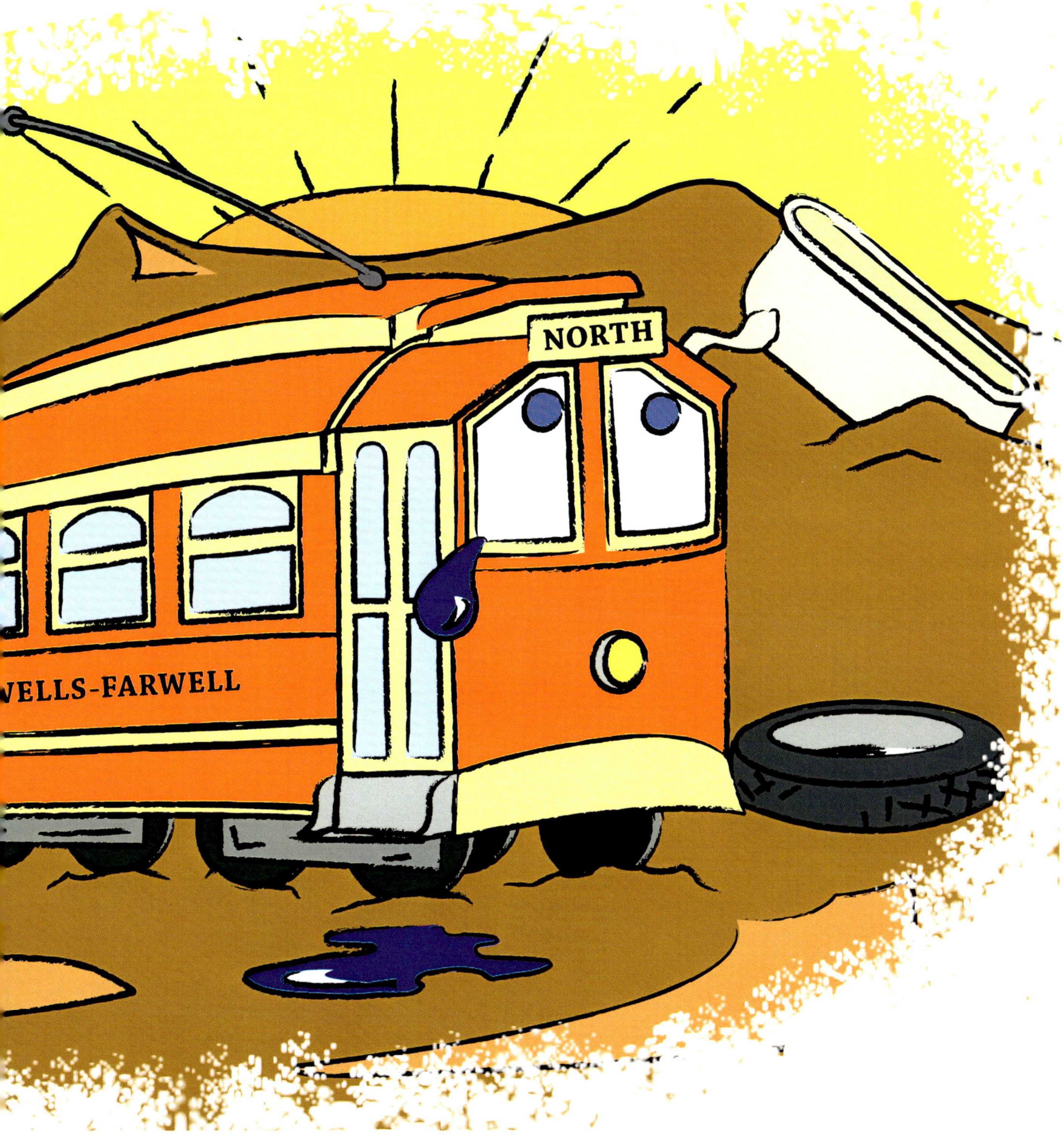
NORTH
WELLS-FARWELL

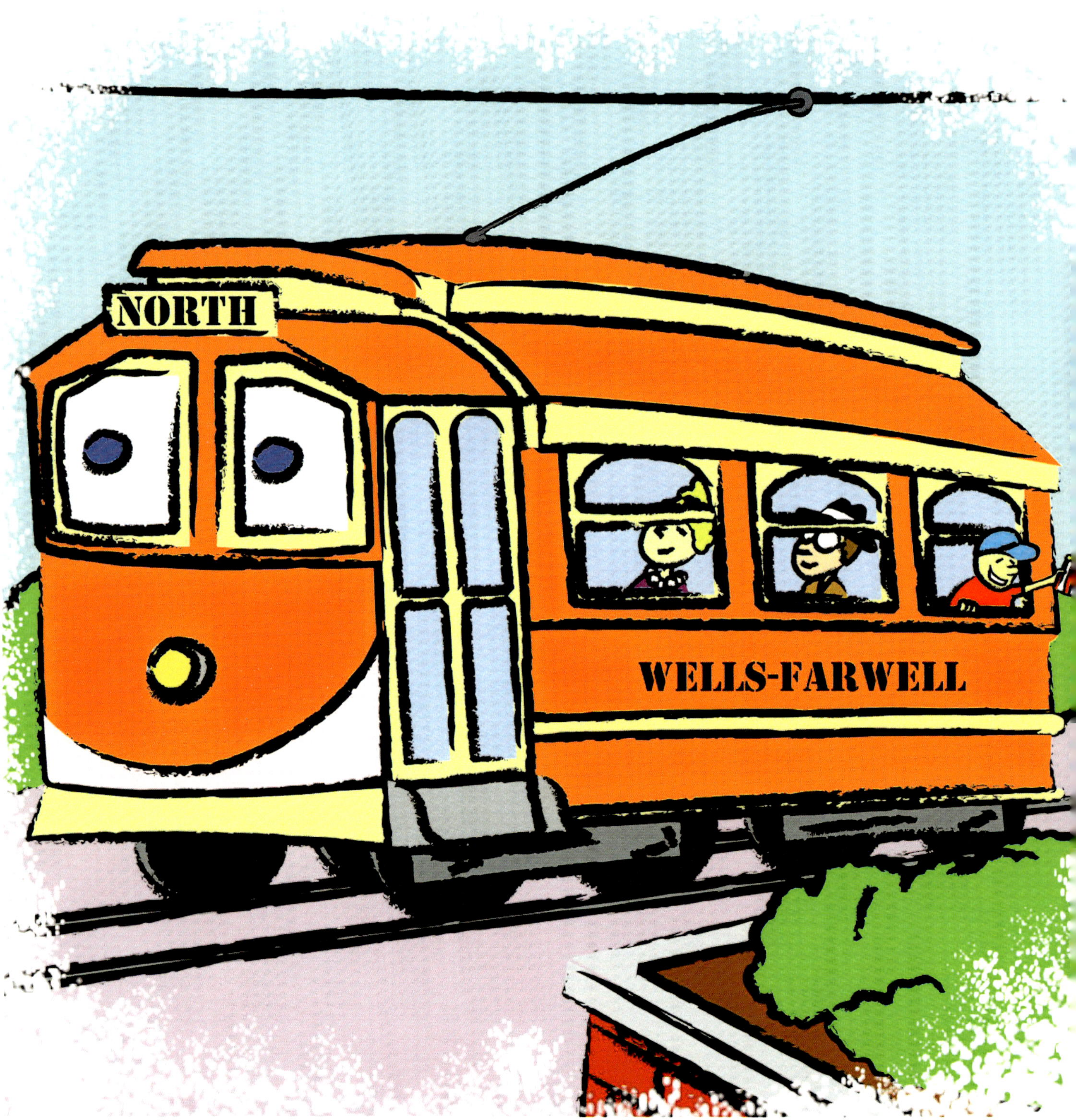
NORTH
WELLS-FARWELL

But Gary had not ridden on him in many, many years. As a matter of fact, no one had ridden on him in many, many years.

So, Al just sat in the scrap yard, and waited, and cried. He could not imagine anyone not wanting to ride on him anymore.

He spent many hours carrying passengers up and down Wells Street every day. He could remember the joy he gave them, as they traveled up and down the line. Some were going to work, and others, like Gary, were going to visit their grandparents. Some were going to school. As Gary grew older, he took the trolley to school, too. Sometimes he got on the trolley with his mom, and they went shopping.

The motorman who operated the trolley made sure Al was hosed down with soap and water every night, and ready to go the next morning. Everyone who got on Al would say how nice he looked. Al was so happy back then.

Al had many friends then, too. When the motorman parked him in the car barn at night, he would talk with the other trolleys. His best friend was Kenny. Kenny carried passengers up and down the National Line. He had all kinds of interesting stories to tell.

Most of Kenny's passengers were all draftsman and engineers – very technical people. Kenny always heard about the plans for a new office building that was going up, or a new grocery store being built. Kenny was very proud to carry such important people up and down the line each day.

Al's other friend was named Jack. Jack had the funniest stories to tell each night. Sometimes passengers would get on the trolley, and forget to get off! They had such a good time riding, that they would forget to get off at their stop.

One day, as Jack tells it, Mrs. Huddleston fell asleep on the trolley. She was supposed to get her hair done for a party that night. But she was so comfortable on the trolley that she slept right through to the end of the line.

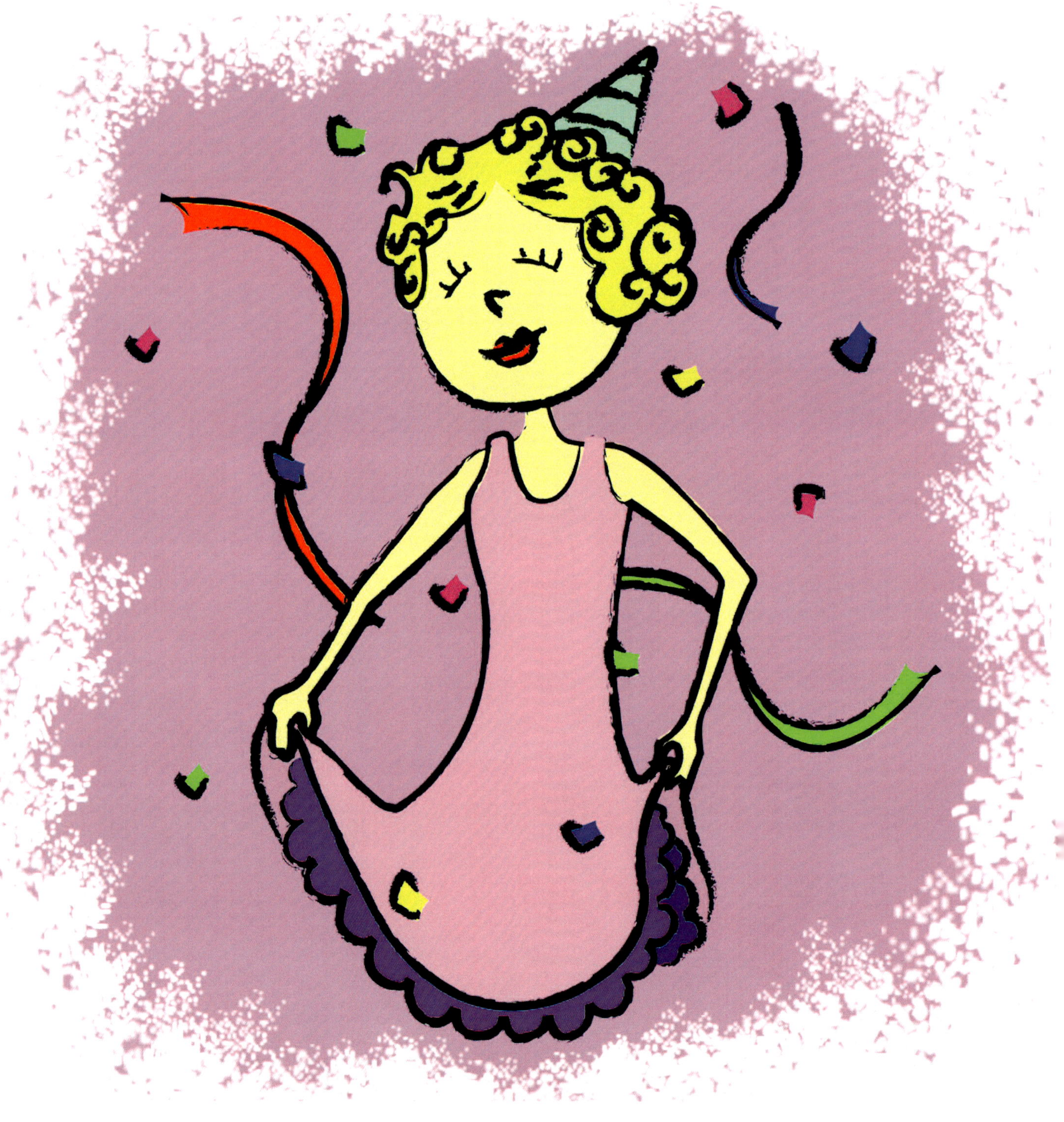

Jack remembers her telling another passenger the story the next day. She had to put pin curlers in her hair when she got home. The pin curlers made her hair curl up real tight. She said Mr. Huddleston told her she looked like a curly poodle, but she went to the party anyway.

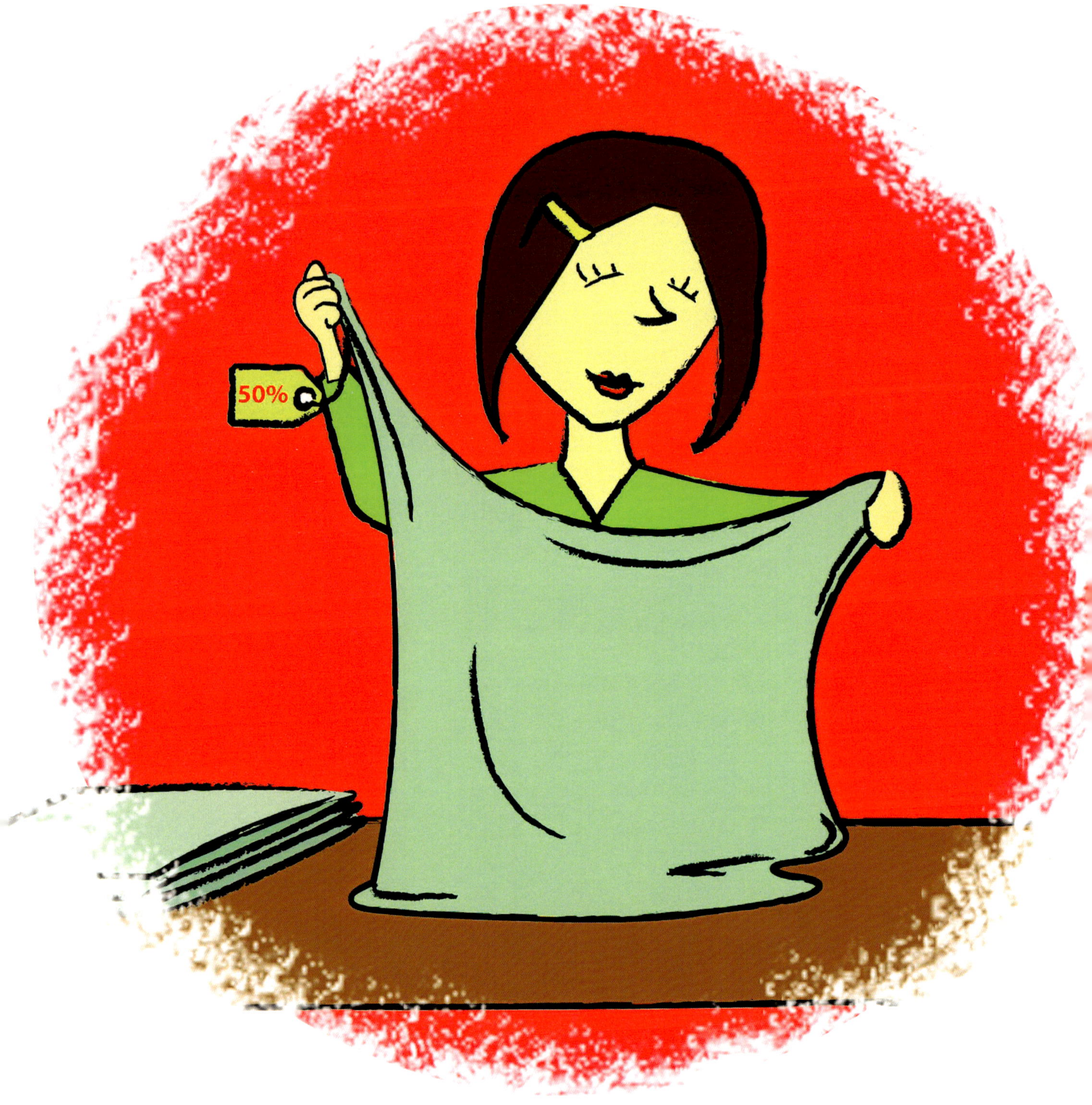
50%

Al also had a friend named Augie. Augie was a friendly trolley. He carried passengers up and down Third Street. He always slowed down so the ladies could catch a ride with him. He told the other trolleys that the ladies were always so nice to him, that he wanted to be nice to them, too.

	He always enjoyed hearing about the things they bought when they got on after shopping. Oh, my, they had so many stories to tell! There was always a BIG SALE somewhere! One day Mrs. Hawbaker bought sheets and pillow cases for 50% off the regular price. She was so excited that she told every lady on the trolley!

Mrs. Clevenger was a teacher. She always bought school supplies for her students. One Saturday, she went to a big sale at the Five and Dime Specialty Store. She bought all of her students pencils, erasers, and writing paper for only a dollar.

Her students were so happy to have new school supplies, that they finished all their school work, and asked Mrs. Clevenger if they could have more writing paper to draw her a picture.

Mrs. Clevenger told the passengers what a wonderful group of students she had.

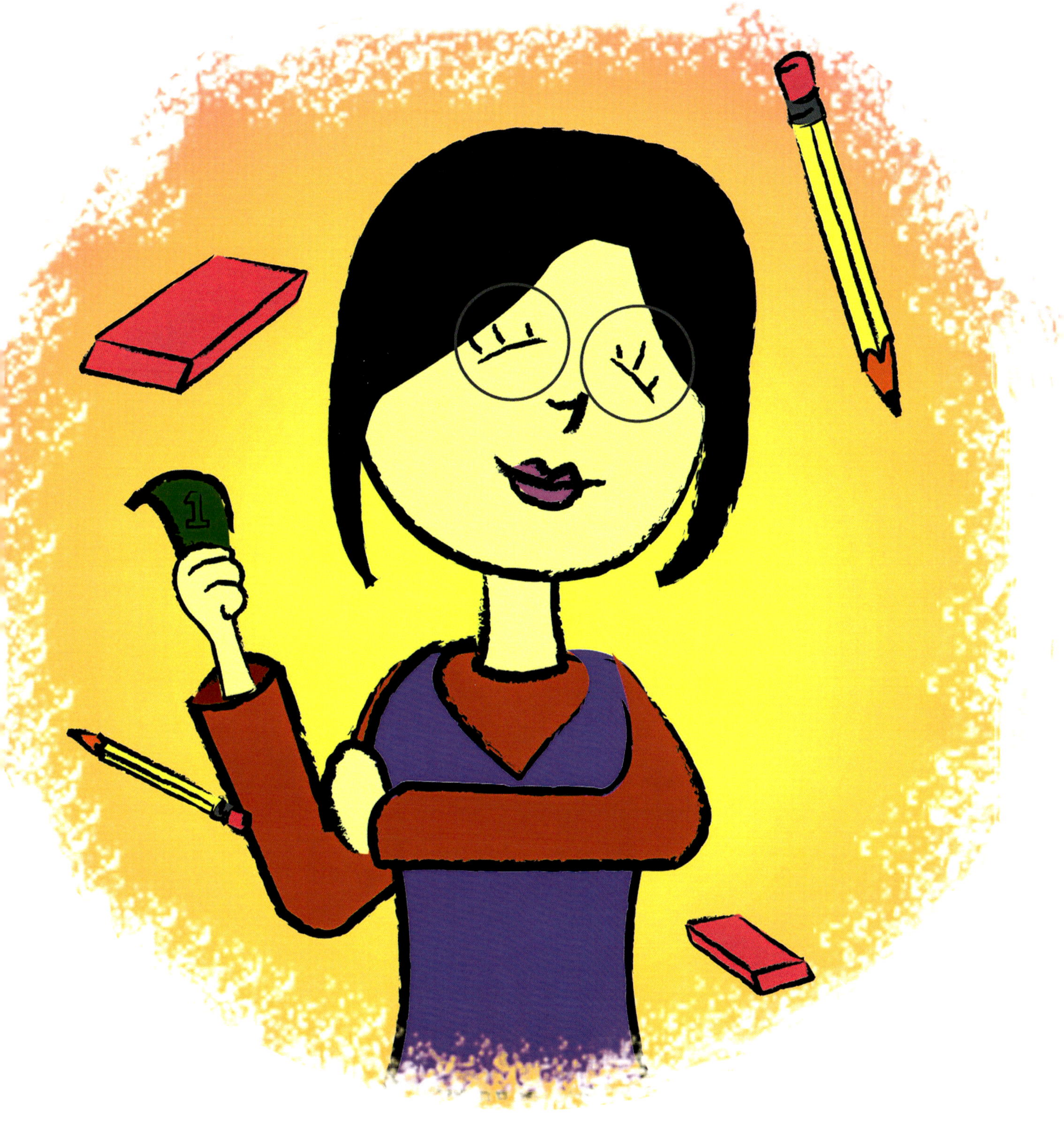
1

These were some of the stories Al heard after the motormen would park them in the car barn, and shut them down for the night. Al missed all these stories, because you see, he was no longer with his friends in the car barn. Everyone had been moved to different places, and he was left alone. He did not even know where they were. But he missed them.

When everyone began buying fast cars, riding on trains, and traveling by airplanes, the trolley cars were no longer needed for transportation. So, they sent them to scrap yards.

Al was sad. His little body was wearing out from just sitting there. He did not know if he would ever carry passengers up and down the Wells Street Line again.

Then, one day, he felt someone tapping on his sides.

Then they were tapping underneath him. Then he felt someone open his doors and hop on the first step.

Who in the world was that? he thought. Was someone going to take a ride on him? Did this person know about trolley cars? All these questions were going through his head, when all of a sudden he heard a man's voice say, "Looks good. I think I will take it."

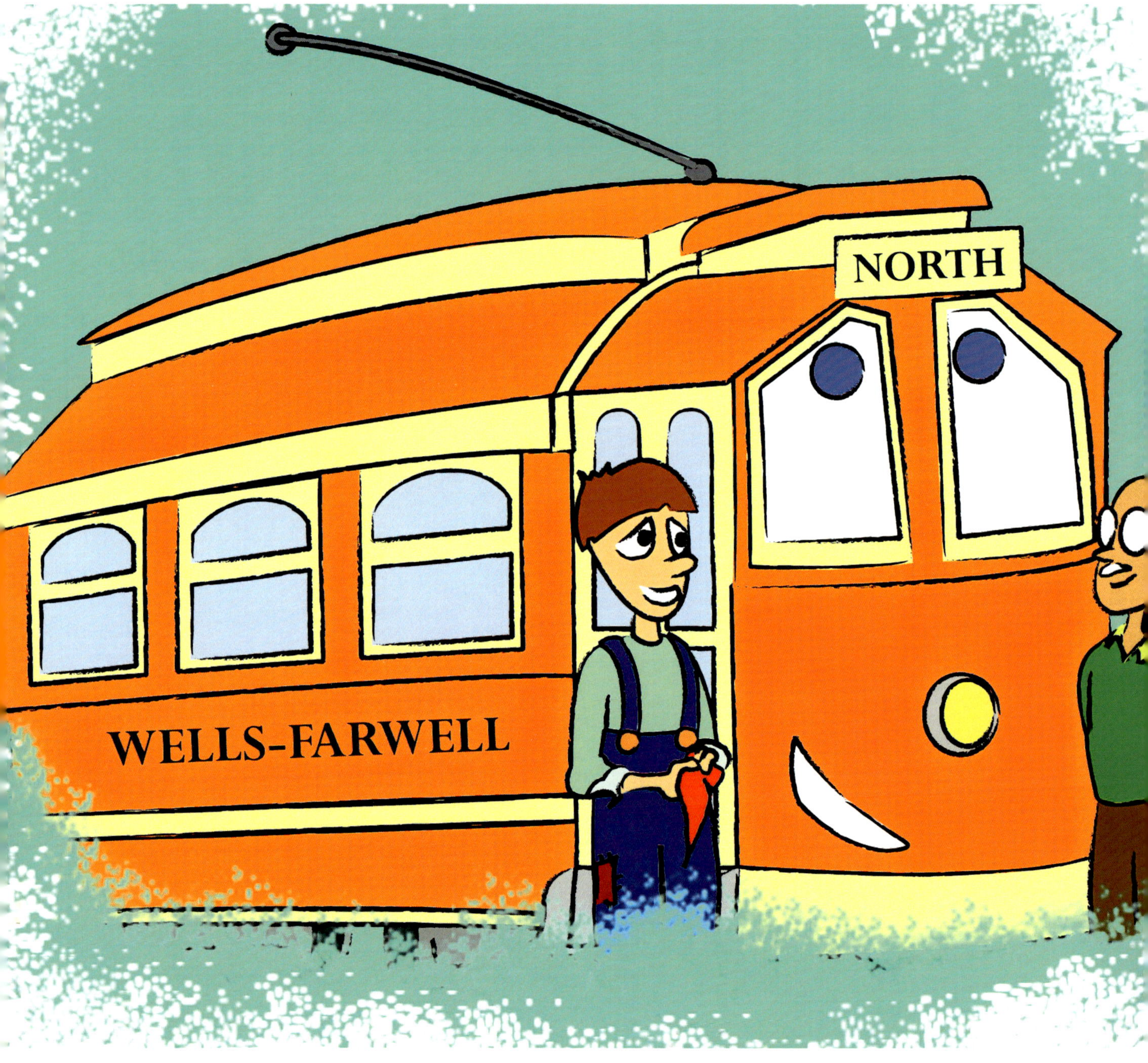
NORTH
WELLS-FARWELL

"Thank you, Gary," said another man's voice, "you won't be disappointed."

Well, what was that all about? thought Al. What looked good? And what was this person going to take?

"I'll have a crane and a flatbed truck come by tomorrow, if that's okay with you," said Gary.

"Sure, that will be fine," replied the second man.

Hmmm, thought Al. A crane . . . a flatbed truck . . . tomorrow . . . Gary . . . GARY? Could this be my old friend, Gary? The kid who used to ride on me all the time? The kid who called me Al?

Al got so excited that he could not sleep that night. Was this really the little boy, Gary? Was he a man now, and was he going to take me somewhere for a ride? Al tossed and turned all night, thinking about Gary and where Gary was going to take him.

Oh, boy, he thought. Gary is going to take me on the trolley tracks and let people ride on me everyday. It will be just like old times, thought Al.

Well, the very next day, a man pulled up in front of Al and began fiddling with some chains on his flatbed truck. He pulled on them, and they made a clinkety-clankety noise.

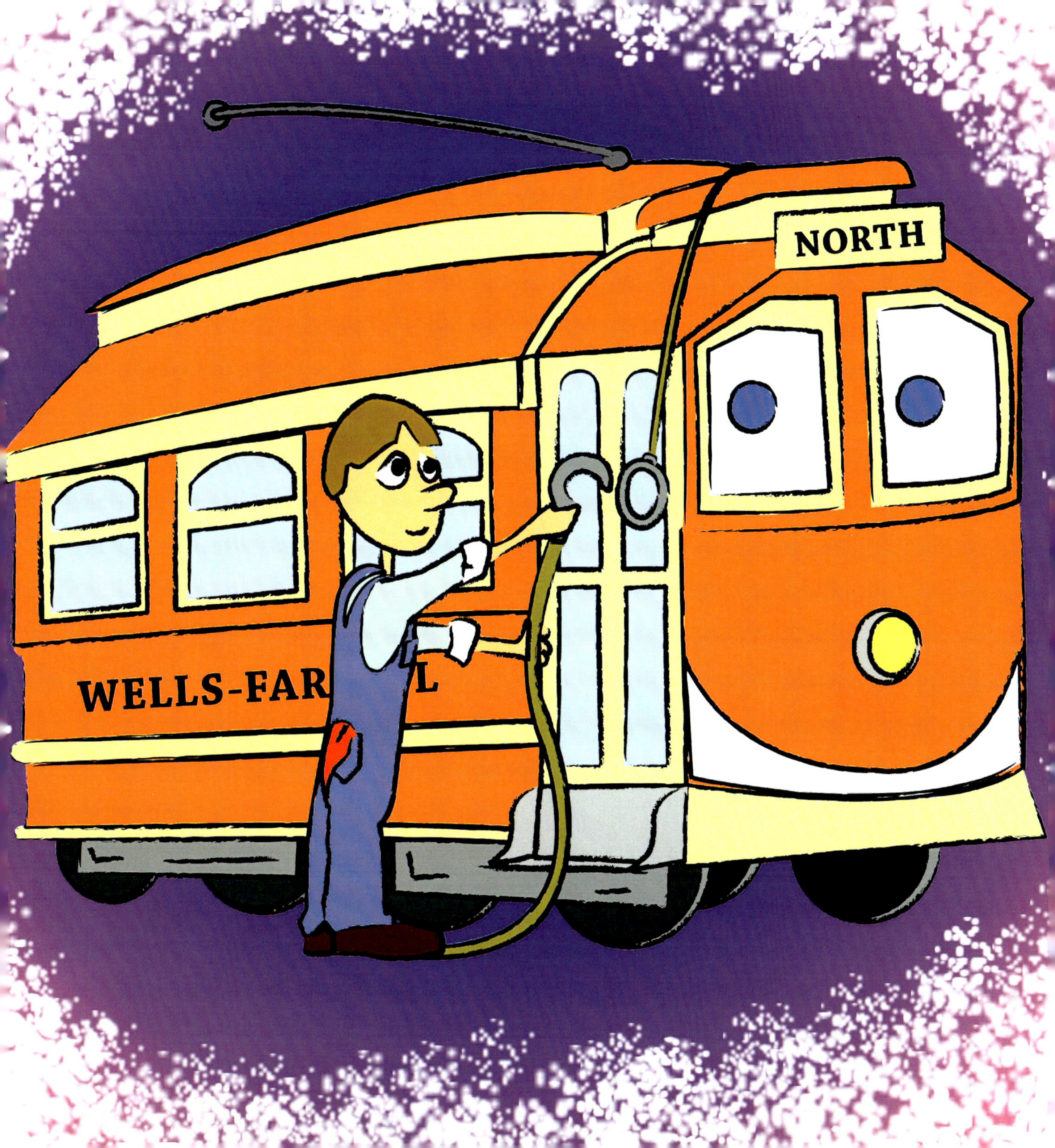
NORTH
WELLS-FAR

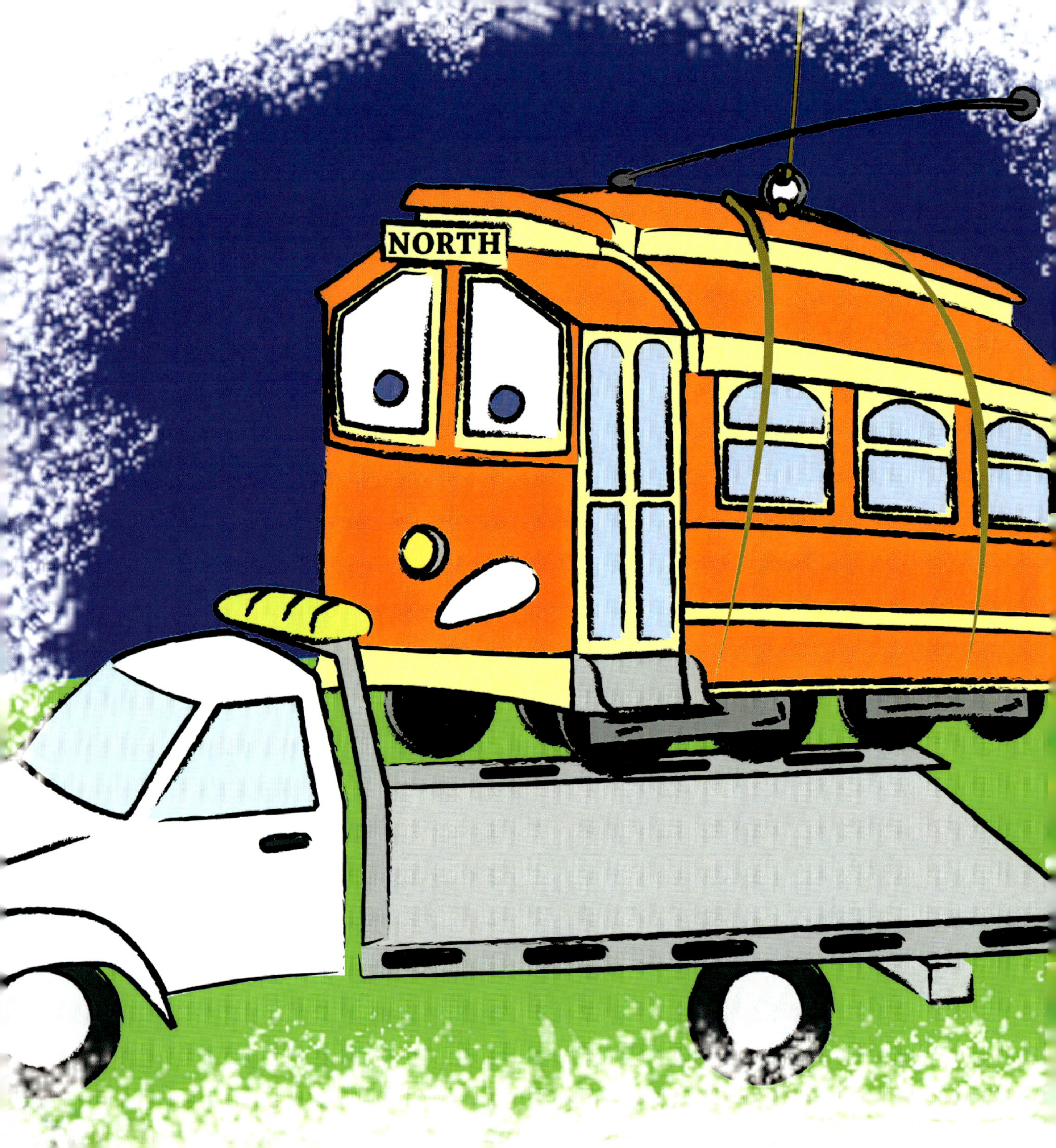
NORTH

Then he lay down on the ground near Al, and began hooking up the chains to Al's front. Al laughed, because he thought it tickled!

Then a man in a crane pulled up, and they both began to talk. The next thing Al knew, he was being lifted up and put on the flatbed truck.

Yikes! thought Al. This feels really weird. Then the man got in his truck, started it up, and began pulling away.

W-e-e-e! thought Al. This is fun! After riding for about an hour, the truck driver pulled into a parking lot. He got out, and went into a restaurant. Al waited.

After about another hour, the man returned. He got back in the truck, started it up, and pulled away. Yippee! thought Al. We are on our way again.

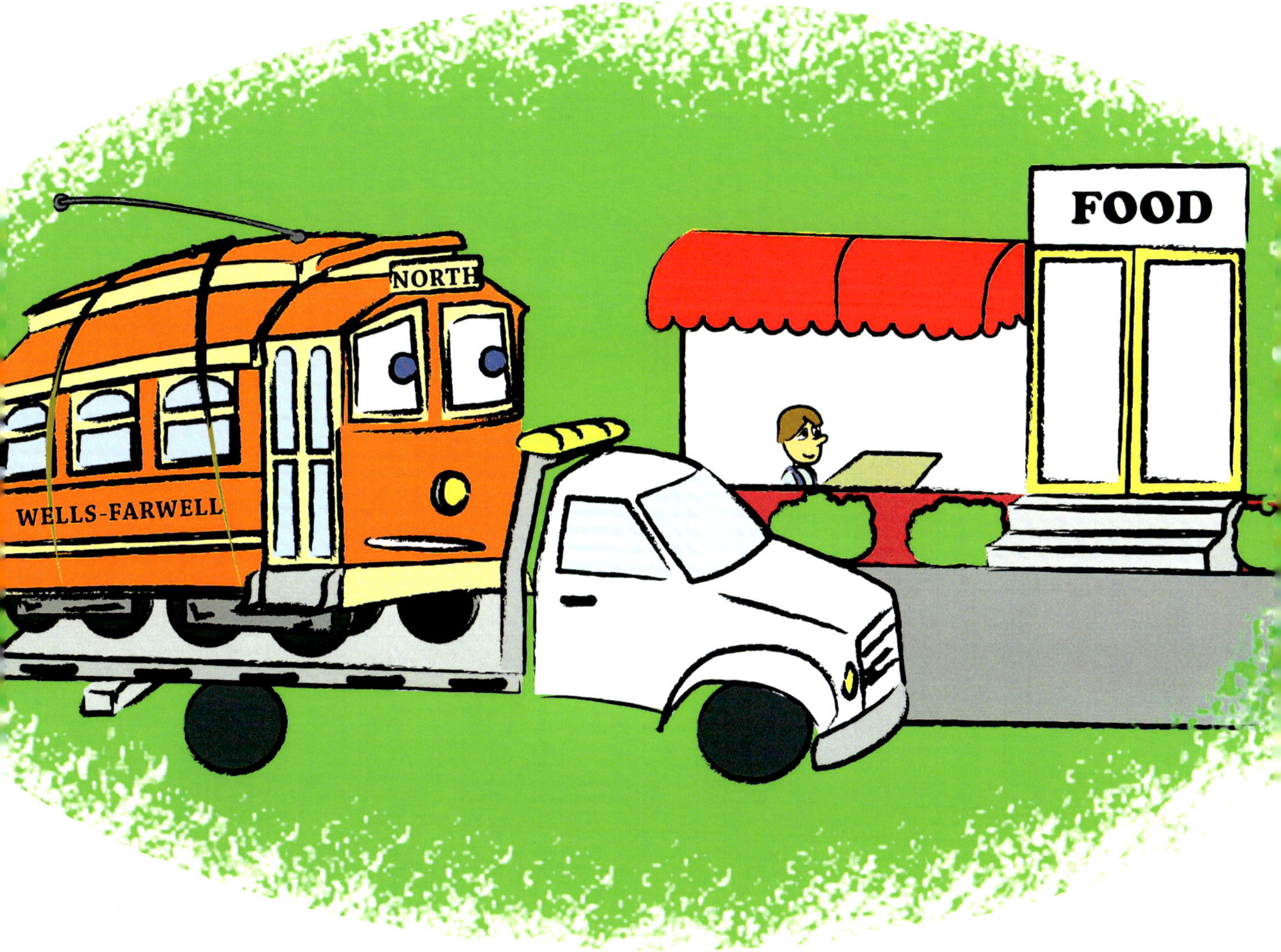
NORTH
WELLS-FARWELL
FOOD

Al rode with the truck driver for another couple of days. Each time, the truck driver would stop, go into a restaurant, and then return. Al thought he ate too much! Sometimes the truck driver would stop and sleep in a motel for the night. Al wanted to get back on the trolley tracks, so he could carry passengers up and down the line again. This truck driver was taking WAY too long! thought Al.

Finally, the truck driver pulled into a big vacant lot and stopped. He got out and went into a small building. When he came out, Gary was walking with him.

Gary! thought Al. Hello! It is so good to see you!

Gary walked up to Al, and looked him over real good. He wanted to make sure there was no damage during the trip. He then directed the truck driver where to park Al, and again, Al had to be lifted off by a crane.

Yow-e-e-e! thought Al.

After he was parked, Gary signed a receipt that the truck driver handed him, and then the driver said, "So, what are you going to do with this old heap?"

Old heap? Who are you calling an old heap? thought Al.

"Oh, I have big plans for him," replied Gary.

"Him?" asked the truck driver.

"Yeah, he's a 'him' I guess," said Gary. "I used to ride him just about everyday when I was a kid in Milwaukee.

"So, I suppose you even gave him a name?" asked the truck driver.

"Yeah, I think I will call him, Al," replied Gary.

"Al? Why Al?" asked the truck driver.

"Well, the motorman who used to drive this trolley was named Al," said Gary, "and whenever I got on the trolley I would always drop a nickel in the fare box, give it a little pat, and say, 'Hello, Al' to the motorman. So, I think I will call him Al."

Oops! thought Al. I thought my name was Al all these years, and it was really the motorman's name! Ha! Ha! Ha! I wonder if my old friends thought the same thing? Their names were probably their motorman's name, too. Ha! Ha! Ha! That is really funny, thought Al.

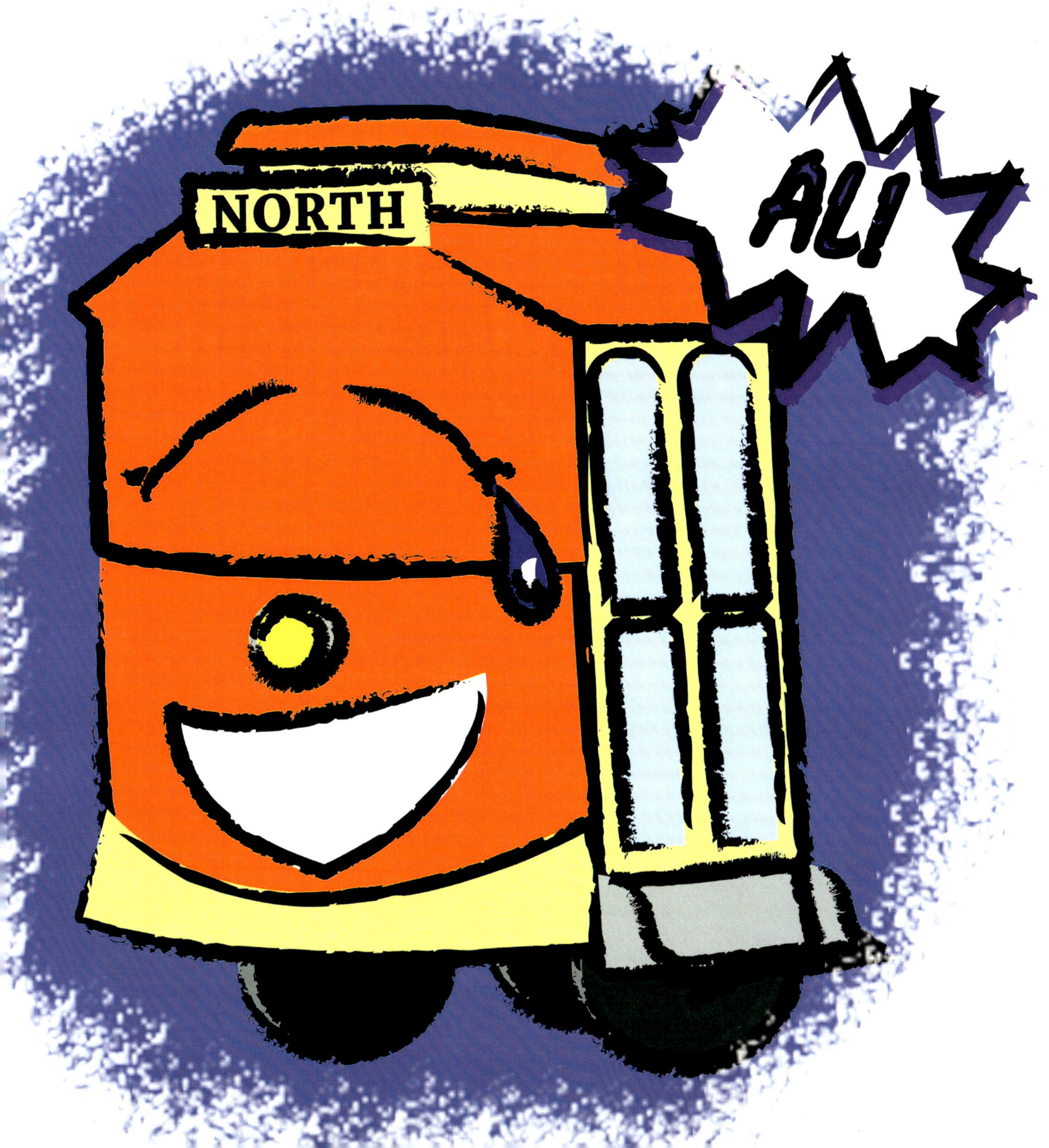
NORTH
ALI!

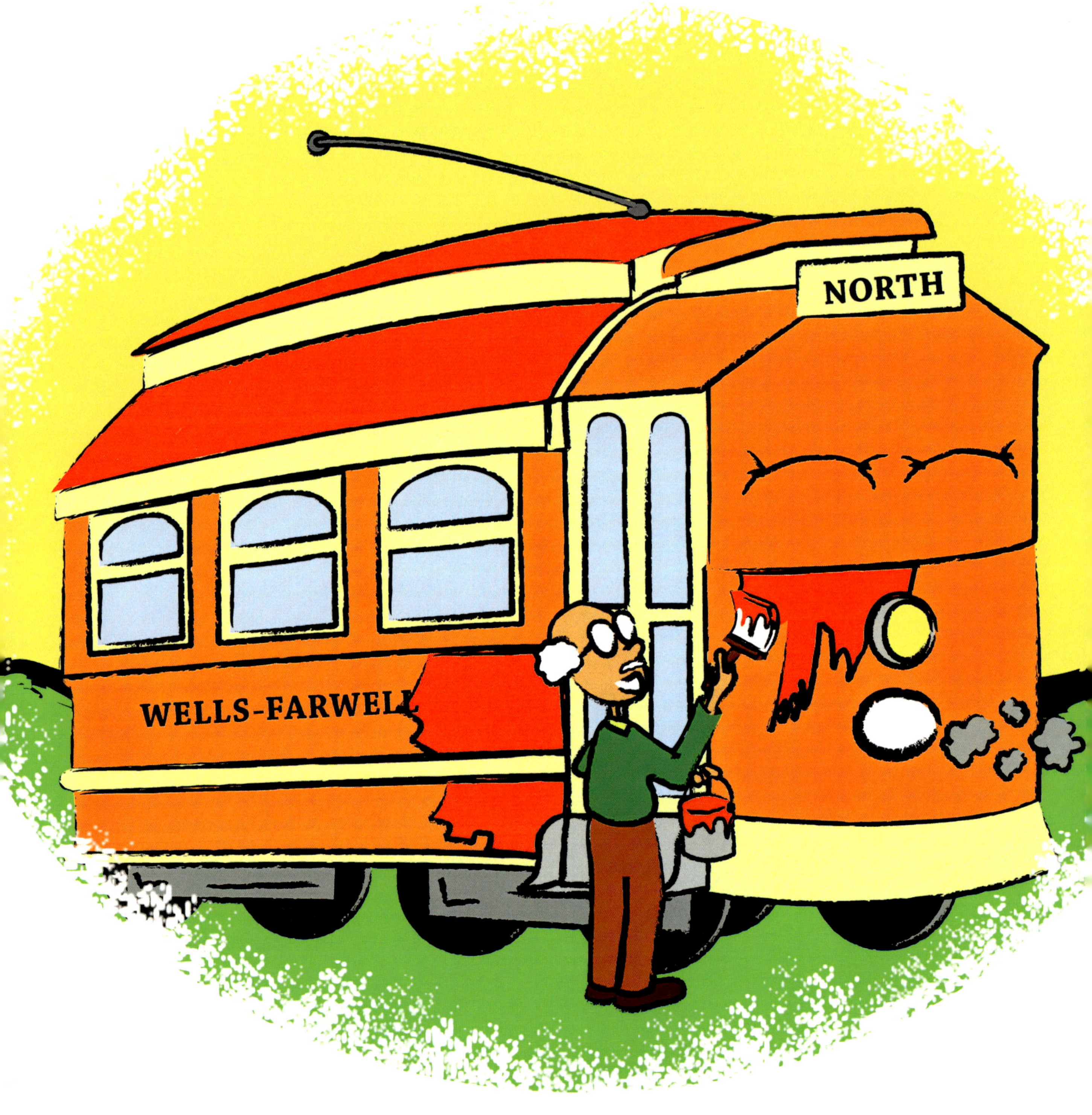
NORTH
WELLS-FARWELL

"Well, good luck, buddy," said the truck driver.

"Thanks," replied Gary.

The truck driver drove off, and Gary began scraping down some of Al's paint from his body.

Ouch! Ooh! E-e-e! Oh! thought Al, as Gary began scraping, wiping, cleaning and fixing him up. What was he doing all that for? thought Al. I am just a little bit dusty.

Well, Gary thought he was more than just a little bit dusty. Over the next couple of days, Gary did all kinds of repair work on Al. After everything was scraped, wiped, and cleaned, Gary began painting Al.

Al started coughing when Gary began to paint, but after awhile, Gary stood back and said, "There. You look as good as new."

Do I? Do I, really? thought Al. Okay, now I am ready to carry passengers again!

Al was so excited that he could not sleep that night, either! Oh, boy! Who was going to ride him first? What trolley line was he going to travel on? Were all the new people going to have as much fun as the other people did? He was so happy.

The next day Gary came to the vacant lot with a bunch of people. Al thought some of them looked familiar by the way they were dressed, and by the papers they were carrying in their hands. Why, they looked just like Kenny's old friends who rode with him. They were just like Kenny's old friends. They were draftsman and engineers.

Everyone got busy measuring the land and measuring Al. They spent hours doing all kinds of measuring, drawing, talking, and deciding. What was all this about? thought Al. Why did Gary need all these people just to get me up and running again?

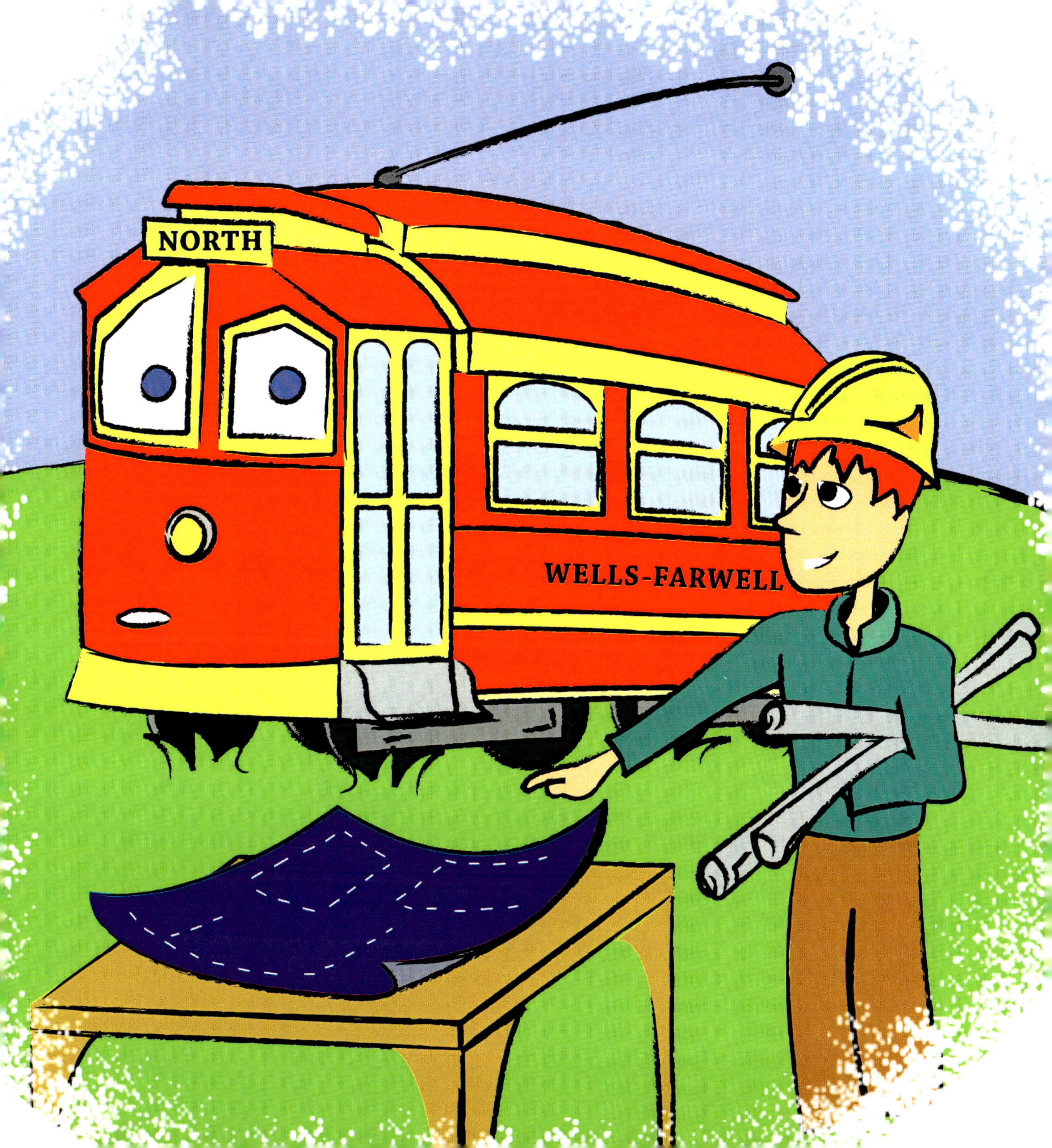
NORTH
WELLS-FARWELL

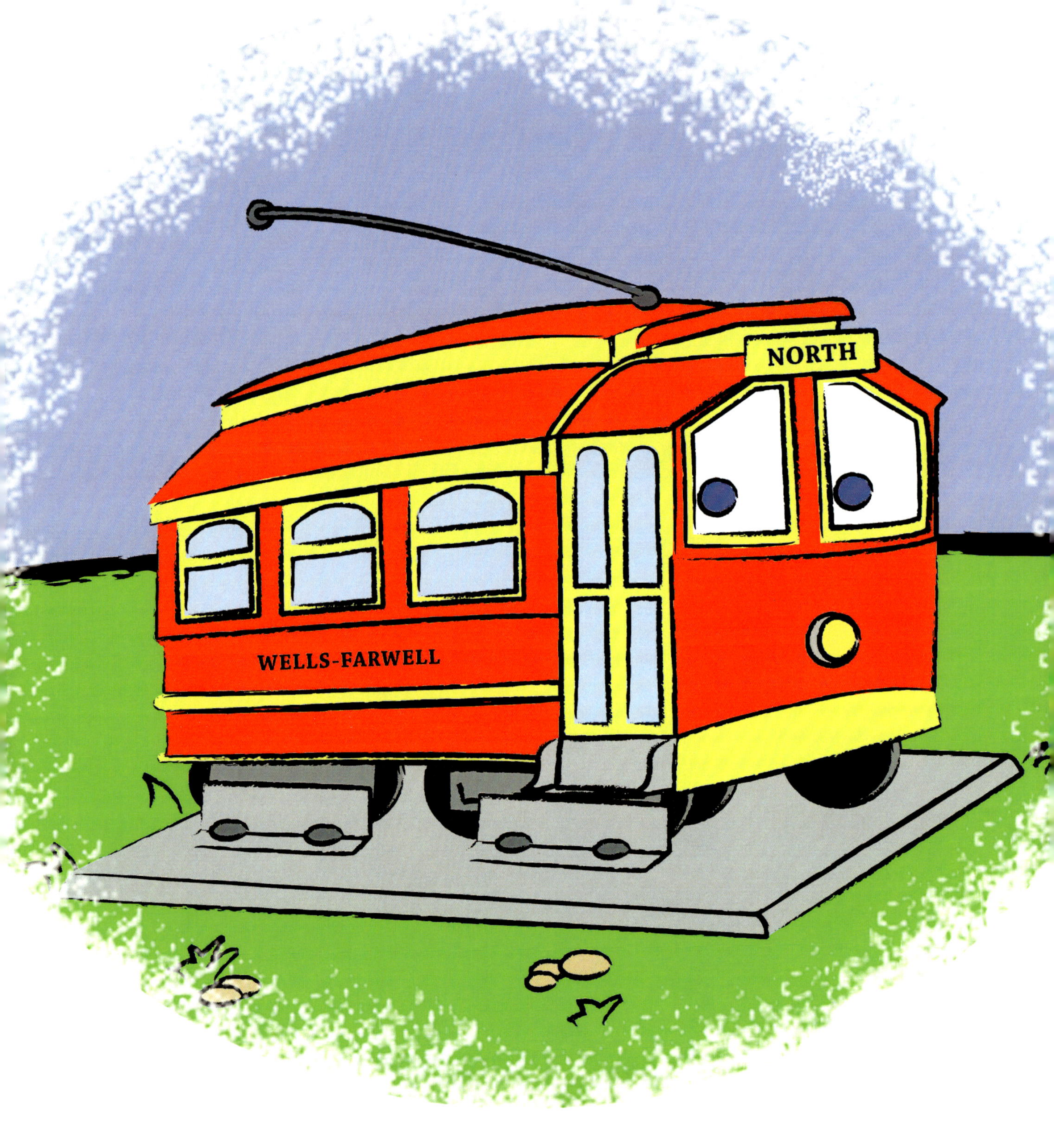
NORTH
WELLS-FARWELL

Another few days went by, and then everyone left. Al was left alone again. What was going on now? thought Al. He sat and waited, and waited, and waited.

A few days later, Gary returned with lots more people, and a crane. A crane? thought Al. What is he doing with another crane? Is he moving me again?

Everyone got busy, and before Al knew it, he had been lifted up, set on a slab of concrete, and bolted down! Bolted down? How could he carry passengers up and down the line if he was bolted down? thought Al.

The next thing he felt, were people going in and out of him. They were setting up something. He did not know what, but it felt strange. This went on for several days. What were they doing? thought Al.
    Then, to Al's surprise, one whole side of him had been removed by workers, and another section added onto him. It looked like some kind of a room!
    Workers then began working in the new room and adding all kinds of machinery, pots and pans, and hooking up gas and water. Al was really confused by all of this. He knew you did not need gas or water to run a trolley, but he could not figure out why they did not know that.

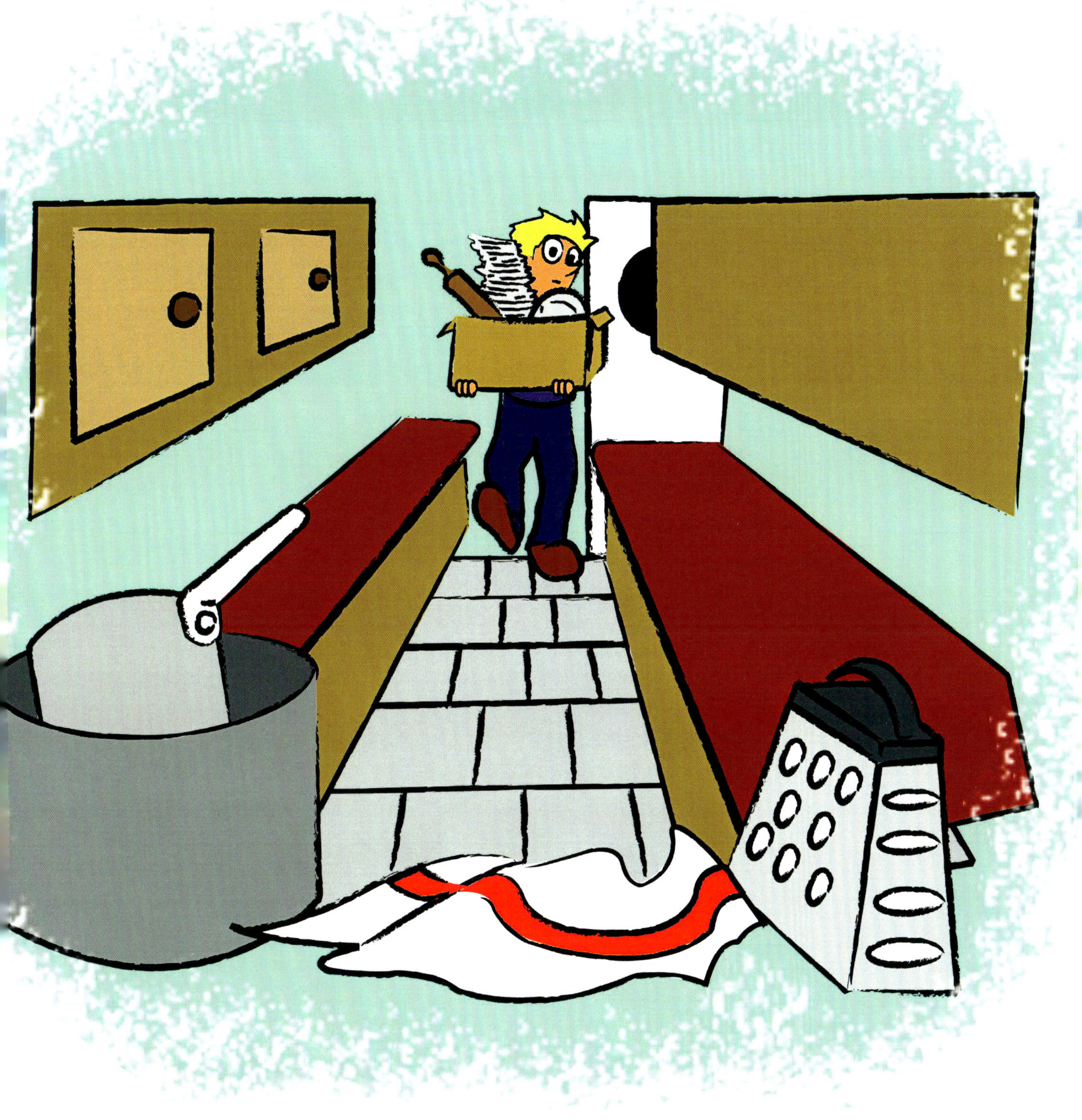

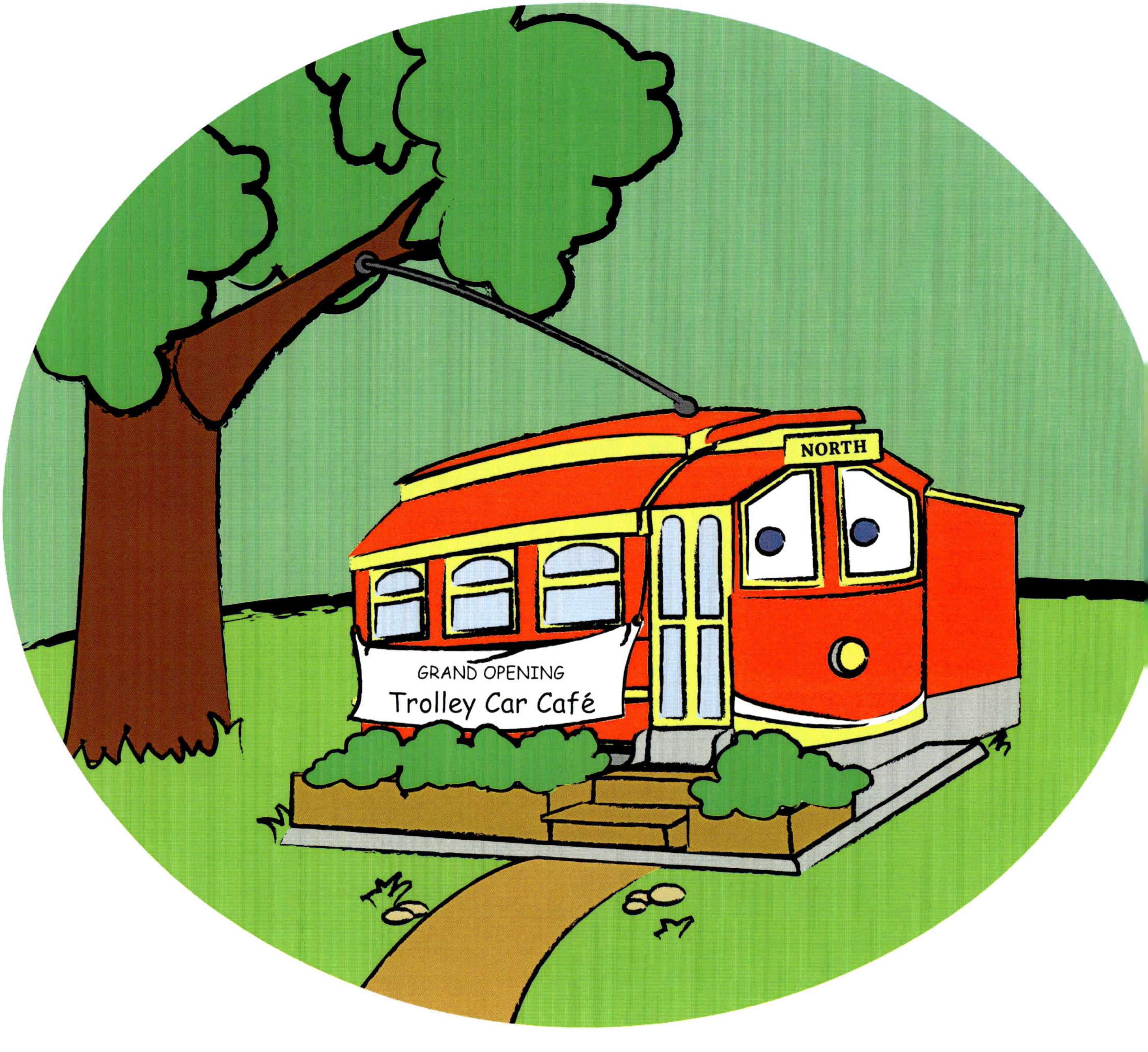
NORTH
GRAND OPENING
Trolley Car Café

Well, before long, Gary came back with a couple of workers, and they put up a huge banner all across one side of Al. A banner? What was the banner for? thought Al. Trolleys don't wear banners. Was this a banner saying, "All Aboard" or what? Al was very confused.

Then he heard Gary talking to some of the other workers. "How do you like the sign?" Gary asked. "It looks pretty good, huh?"

"Yeah," said one of the workers, and he began reading it. "Grand Opening! The Trolley Car Café."

The what? thought Al. A café? A trolley car café? What in the world had Gary done to him? I am a . . . café? I am a . . . and his thoughts trailed off, because he was so ashamed.

Then everyone left, and he was alone again. He did not know what to think. Was this what Gary had planned for him? Was he no longer going to ride up and down the trolley tracks, taking passengers from place to place? What was going to become of him? thought Al.

The next morning, the sun came shining brightly through Al's beautiful red checkered curtains. Curtains? thought Al. I have curtains? Oh, no! I am doomed!

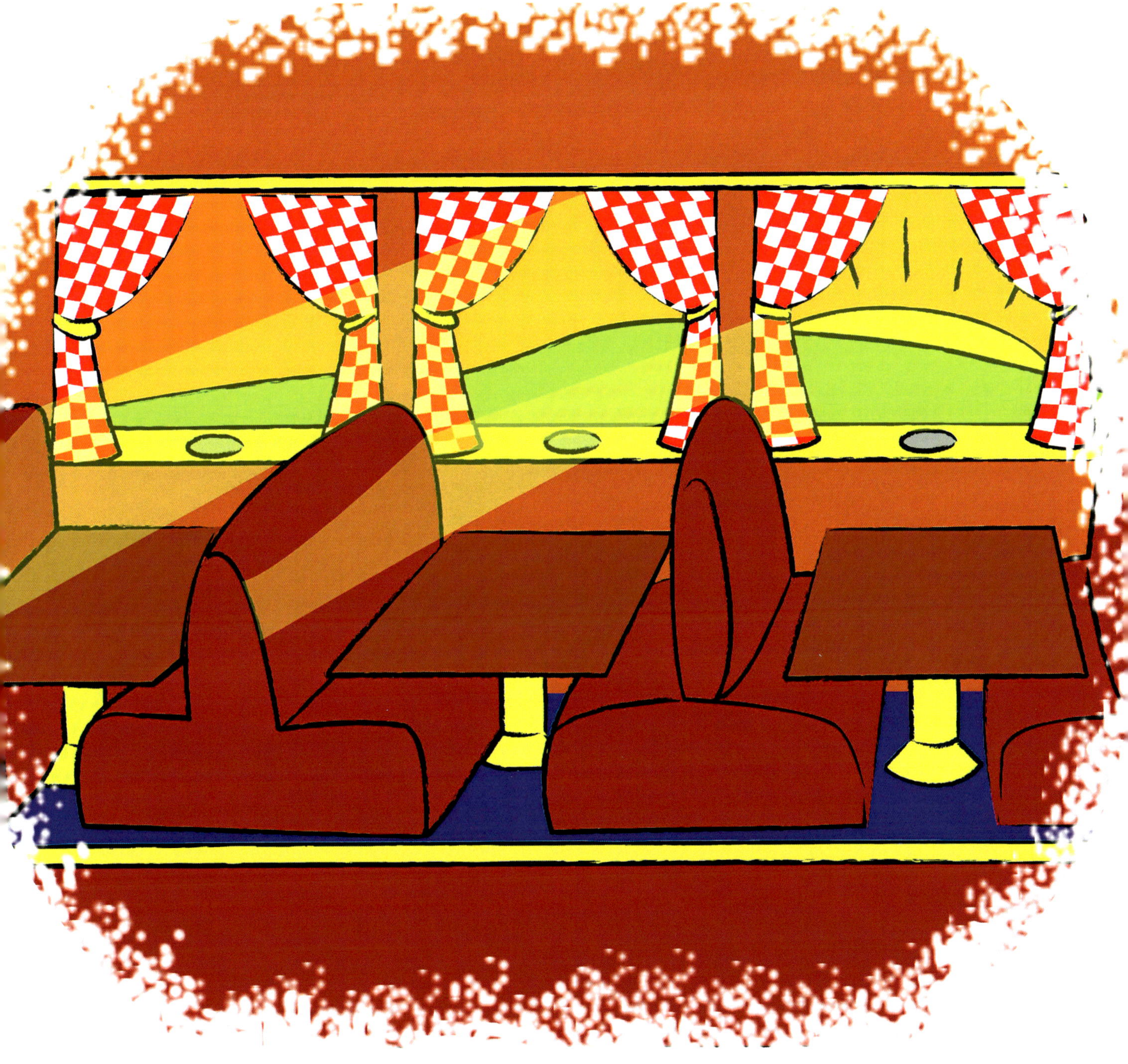

Then, Gary opened the doors, and people began climbing aboard. For what? thought Al. I can't go anywhere. The next thing he heard, were people talking about what they wanted to eat for breakfast. Then Al smelled the most wonderful smells coming from the kitchen? The KITCHEN? Oh, yeah, that's right. I am a café! thought Al. People come here to eat! No wonder it smells so good!

   It not only smelled good, but people were talking and laughing, and telling all kinds of stories as they ate their breakfast. This was so much fun, thought Al.

   Some of the older customers began telling stories about the trolleys they rode on as kids. Al was so shocked when one of them started telling about riding on "Jack." Of course, they didn't call him "Jack", but Al knew who they were talking about by the street they said they rode on.

   It wasn't only the older customers who were talking. Some of the younger ones wanted to know all about the trolleys. They had never ridden on one, because the trolleys were all sent to scrap yards long before they were born. But they still wanted to know about them.

Al could not believe his ears! Everyone was having such a good time, eating, talking, and telling stories about . . . about . . . well, about trolleys!

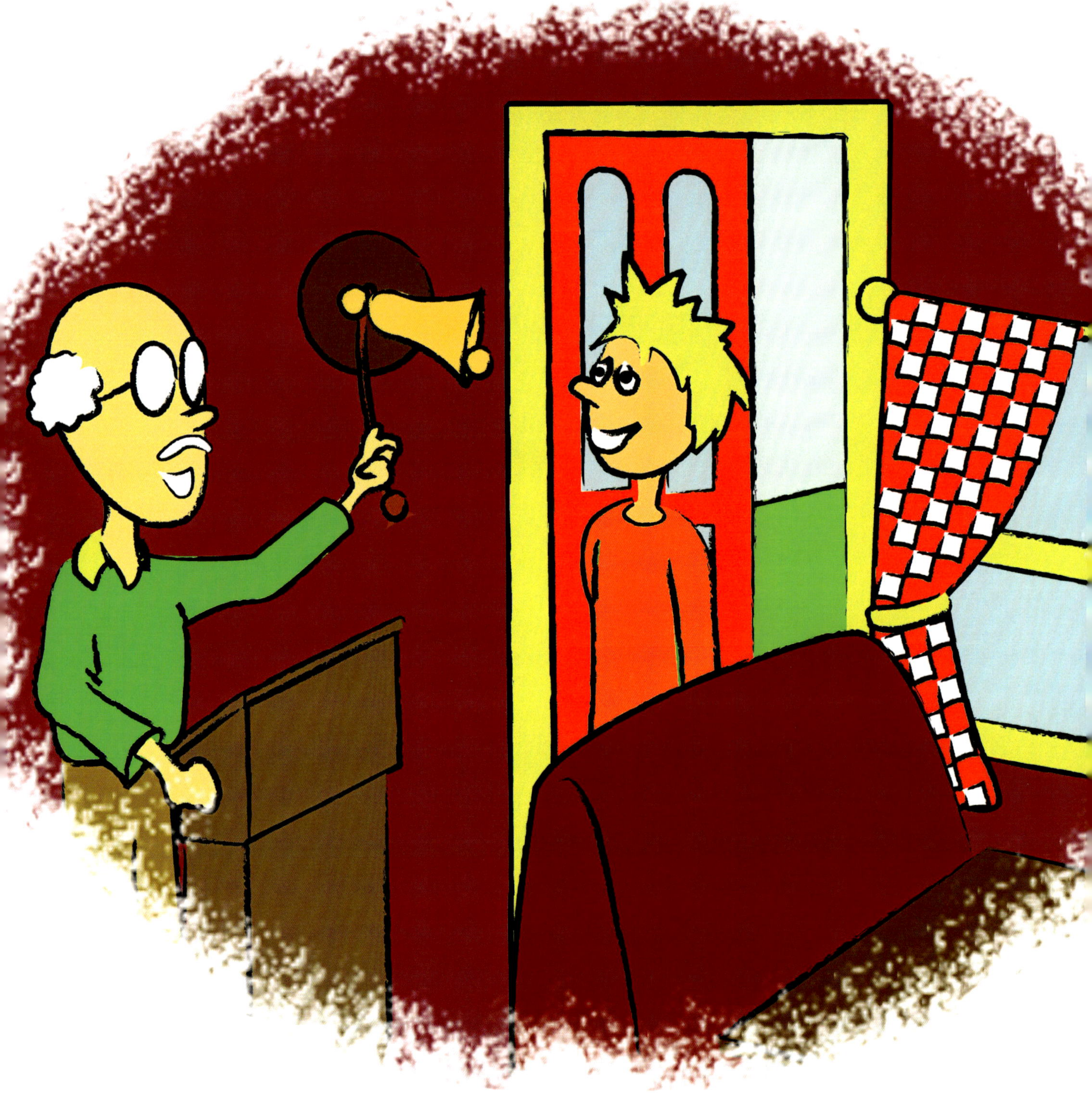

Oh, how happy he was. Gary told some of the customers that he did what he thought was best for Al. Since there were no longer any trolley tracks, or trolleys running, except in trolley museums, Gary thought that Al would be happier here, instead of sitting in an old scrap yard.

Al spent many, many hours listening to all the wonderful people come in and out to eat. They came in for breakfast, lunch, and dinner. They were so happy to visit him, and he was so happy that they did. He would never cry about being lonely again. He thought, the next time I cry, it will be for tears of joy.

But something was missing, thought Al. He could not remember what it was, but something was definitely missing.

Just then, the door opened, a man walked in, and Gary yelled, "Congratulations! You are my 100th customer!" And Gary began ringing the trolley car bell.

That's it! thought Al. That's what was missing—my bell!

When everyone had finished eating, and the workers had washed all the dishes, Gary turned out the lights, patted the fare box, and said, "Good night, Al. It's good to have you back again."

Al watched Gary walk away, as the stars twinkled brightly in the sky, and the moon shown down upon the little forgotten trolley. He sat very still. He was very, very quiet. But this time he knew someone would visit him again!

Then he sighed, and a little tear of joy trickled down his cheek.

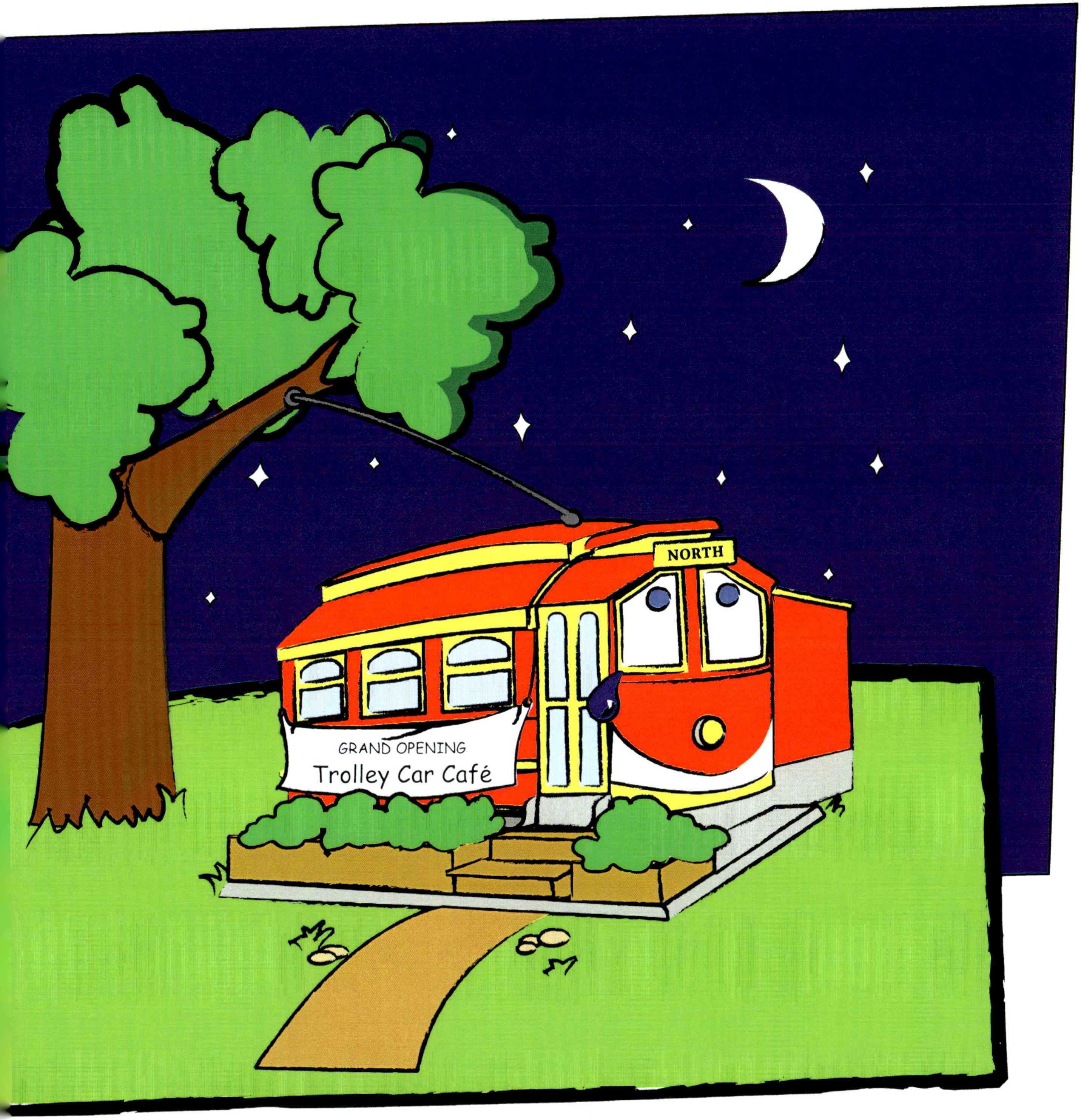
NORTH
GRAND OPENING
Trolley Car Café

THE END